50 Quick Pickling Recipes for Home

By: Kelly Johnson

Table of Contents

- Quick Pickled Cucumbers
- Pickled Red Onions
- Quick Pickled Jalapeños
- Pickled Carrots
- Quick Pickled Radishes
- Pickled Garlic
- Pickled Cauliflower
- Quick Pickled Beets
- Pickled Green Tomatoes
- Quick Pickled Peppers
- Pickled Asparagus
- Quick Pickled Zucchini
- Pickled Mushrooms
- Quick Pickled Watermelon Rind
- Pickled Brussels Sprouts
- Quick Pickled Cherries
- Pickled Carrots and Daikon
- Quick Pickled Ginger
- Pickled Shrimp
- Quick Pickled Apples
- Pickled Fennel
- Quick Pickled Lemons
- Pickled Eggplant
- Quick Pickled Bell Peppers
- Pickled Okra
- Quick Pickled Celery
- Pickled Dill Carrots
- Quick Pickled Pineapple
- Pickled Baby Corn
- Quick Pickled Artichokes
- Pickled Scallions
- Quick Pickled Thai Basil
- Pickled Radish Slaw
- Quick Pickled Snow Peas
- Pickled Baby Beets

- Quick Pickled Cabbage
- Pickled Cilantro Lime Carrots
- Quick Pickled Green Beans
- Pickled Sweet Potatoes
- Quick Pickled Mustard Greens
- Pickled Daikon
- Quick Pickled Lemongrass
- Pickled Fiddleheads
- Quick Pickled Habaneros
- Pickled Turnips
- Quick Pickled Mango
- Pickled Seaweed
- Quick Pickled Cabbage and Carrots
- Pickled Coconut
- Quick Pickled Summer Squash

Quick Pickled Cucumbers

Ingredients:

- 2 cups thinly sliced cucumbers
- 1 cup white vinegar
- 1/2 cup water
- 1/4 cup sugar
- 1 tablespoon salt
- 1 teaspoon dill seeds (optional)

Instructions:

1. **Prepare the Brine**
   In a saucepan, combine vinegar, water, sugar, and salt. Heat until the sugar dissolves.
2. **Pack the Cucumbers**
   Place sliced cucumbers in a jar. Add dill seeds if using.
3. **Add the Brine**
   Pour the hot brine over the cucumbers.
4. **Cool and Refrigerate**
   Let cool, then refrigerate for at least 1 hour before serving.

Pickled Red Onions

Ingredients:

- 1 large red onion, thinly sliced
- 1 cup apple cider vinegar
- 1/2 cup water
- 1 tablespoon sugar
- 1 teaspoon salt
- 1/2 teaspoon black peppercorns (optional)

Instructions:

1. **Prepare the Brine**
   In a saucepan, combine vinegar, water, sugar, and salt. Heat until dissolved.
2. **Pack the Onions**
   Place sliced onions in a jar. Add peppercorns if using.
3. **Add the Brine**
   Pour the hot brine over the onions.
4. **Cool and Refrigerate**
   Let cool, then refrigerate for at least 1 hour before serving.

Quick Pickled Jalapeños

Ingredients:

- 1 cup sliced jalapeños
- 1 cup white vinegar
- 1/2 cup water
- 1 tablespoon sugar
- 1 teaspoon salt

Instructions:

1. **Prepare the Brine**
   In a saucepan, combine vinegar, water, sugar, and salt. Heat until the sugar dissolves.
2. **Pack the Jalapeños**
   Place sliced jalapeños in a jar.
3. **Add the Brine**
   Pour the hot brine over the jalapeños.
4. **Cool and Refrigerate**
   Let cool, then refrigerate for at least 1 hour before serving.

Pickled Carrots

Ingredients:

- 2 cups sliced carrots
- 1 cup white vinegar
- 1/2 cup water
- 1 tablespoon sugar
- 1 teaspoon salt
- 1 teaspoon coriander seeds (optional)

Instructions:

1. **Prepare the Brine**
   In a saucepan, combine vinegar, water, sugar, and salt. Heat until dissolved.
2. **Pack the Carrots**
   Place sliced carrots in a jar. Add coriander seeds if using.
3. **Add the Brine**
   Pour the hot brine over the carrots.
4. **Cool and Refrigerate**
   Let cool, then refrigerate for at least 1 hour before serving.

Quick Pickled Radishes

Ingredients:

- 2 cups thinly sliced radishes
- 1 cup rice vinegar
- 1/2 cup water
- 1 tablespoon sugar
- 1 teaspoon salt

Instructions:

1. **Prepare the Brine**
   In a saucepan, combine vinegar, water, sugar, and salt. Heat until dissolved.
2. **Pack the Radishes**
   Place sliced radishes in a jar.
3. **Add the Brine**
   Pour the hot brine over the radishes.
4. **Cool and Refrigerate**
   Let cool, then refrigerate for at least 1 hour before serving.

Pickled Garlic

Ingredients:

- 1 cup peeled garlic cloves
- 1 cup white vinegar
- 1/2 cup water
- 1 tablespoon salt
- 1 tablespoon sugar
- 1 teaspoon red pepper flakes (optional)

Instructions:

1. **Prepare the Brine**
   In a saucepan, combine vinegar, water, salt, and sugar. Heat until dissolved.
2. **Pack the Garlic**
   Place garlic cloves in a jar. Add red pepper flakes if using.
3. **Add the Brine**
   Pour the hot brine over the garlic.
4. **Cool and Refrigerate**
   Let cool, then refrigerate for at least 1 week before serving.

Pickled Cauliflower

Ingredients:

- 2 cups cauliflower florets
- 1 cup white vinegar
- 1/2 cup water
- 1 tablespoon sugar
- 1 teaspoon salt
- 1 teaspoon mustard seeds (optional)

Instructions:

1. **Prepare the Brine**
   In a saucepan, combine vinegar, water, sugar, and salt. Heat until dissolved.
2. **Pack the Cauliflower**
   Place cauliflower florets in a jar. Add mustard seeds if using.
3. **Add the Brine**
   Pour the hot brine over the cauliflower.
4. **Cool and Refrigerate**
   Let cool, then refrigerate for at least 1 hour before serving.

Quick Pickled Beets

Ingredients:

- 2 cups cooked and sliced beets
- 1 cup apple cider vinegar
- 1/2 cup water
- 1/4 cup sugar
- 1 teaspoon salt
- 1 teaspoon cinnamon (optional)

Instructions:

1. **Prepare the Brine**
   In a saucepan, combine vinegar, water, sugar, salt, and cinnamon. Heat until dissolved.
2. **Pack the Beets**
   Place sliced beets in a jar.
3. **Add the Brine**
   Pour the hot brine over the beets.
4. **Cool and Refrigerate**
   Let cool, then refrigerate for at least 2 hours before serving.

Pickled Green Tomatoes

Ingredients:

- 2 cups sliced green tomatoes
- 1 cup white vinegar
- 1/2 cup water
- 1 tablespoon sugar
- 1 tablespoon salt
- 1 teaspoon dill seeds (optional)

Instructions:

1. **Prepare the Brine**
   In a saucepan, combine vinegar, water, sugar, and salt. Heat until dissolved.
2. **Pack the Tomatoes**
   Place sliced green tomatoes in a jar. Add dill seeds if using.
3. **Add the Brine**
   Pour the hot brine over the tomatoes.
4. **Cool and Refrigerate**
   Let cool, then refrigerate for at least 24 hours before serving.

Quick Pickled Peppers

Ingredients:

- 2 cups sliced bell peppers
- 1 cup white vinegar
- 1/2 cup water
- 1 tablespoon sugar
- 1 teaspoon salt
- 1/2 teaspoon crushed red pepper (optional)

Instructions:

1. **Prepare the Brine**
   In a saucepan, combine vinegar, water, sugar, and salt. Heat until dissolved.
2. **Pack the Peppers**
   Place sliced peppers in a jar. Add crushed red pepper if using.
3. **Add the Brine**
   Pour the hot brine over the peppers.
4. **Cool and Refrigerate**
   Let cool, then refrigerate for at least 1 hour before serving.

Pickled Asparagus

Ingredients:

- 2 cups asparagus spears
- 1 cup white vinegar
- 1/2 cup water
- 1 tablespoon sugar
- 1 teaspoon salt
- 1 clove garlic (optional)

Instructions:

1. **Prepare the Brine**
   In a saucepan, combine vinegar, water, sugar, and salt. Heat until dissolved.
2. **Pack the Asparagus**
   Place asparagus in a jar. Add garlic if using.
3. **Add the Brine**
   Pour the hot brine over the asparagus.
4. **Cool and Refrigerate**
   Let cool, then refrigerate for at least 2 hours before serving.

Quick Pickled Zucchini

Ingredients:

- 2 cups sliced zucchini
- 1 cup apple cider vinegar
- 1/2 cup water
- 1 tablespoon sugar
- 1 teaspoon salt
- 1 teaspoon dried oregano (optional)

Instructions:

1. **Prepare the Brine**
   In a saucepan, combine vinegar, water, sugar, and salt. Heat until dissolved.
2. **Pack the Zucchini**
   Place sliced zucchini in a jar. Add oregano if using.
3. **Add the Brine**
   Pour the hot brine over the zucchini.
4. **Cool and Refrigerate**
   Let cool, then refrigerate for at least 1 hour before serving.

Pickled Mushrooms

Ingredients:

- 2 cups sliced mushrooms
- 1 cup white vinegar
- 1/2 cup water
- 1 tablespoon sugar
- 1 teaspoon salt
- 1/2 teaspoon thyme (optional)

Instructions:

1. **Prepare the Brine**
   In a saucepan, combine vinegar, water, sugar, and salt. Heat until dissolved.
2. **Pack the Mushrooms**
   Place sliced mushrooms in a jar. Add thyme if using.
3. **Add the Brine**
   Pour the hot brine over the mushrooms.
4. **Cool and Refrigerate**
   Let cool, then refrigerate for at least 2 hours before serving.

Quick Pickled Watermelon Rind

Ingredients:

- 2 cups peeled and cubed watermelon rind
- 1 cup apple cider vinegar
- 1/2 cup water
- 1/2 cup sugar
- 1 teaspoon salt
- 1 teaspoon ground ginger (optional)

Instructions:

1. **Prepare the Brine**
   In a saucepan, combine vinegar, water, sugar, salt, and ginger. Heat until dissolved.
2. **Pack the Rind**
   Place watermelon rind in a jar.
3. **Add the Brine**
   Pour the hot brine over the rind.
4. **Cool and Refrigerate**
   Let cool, then refrigerate for at least 24 hours before serving.

Pickled Brussels Sprouts

Ingredients:

- 2 cups Brussels sprouts, trimmed and halved
- 1 cup white vinegar
- 1/2 cup water
- 1 tablespoon sugar
- 1 teaspoon salt
- 1 teaspoon mustard seeds (optional)

Instructions:

1. **Prepare the Brine**
   In a saucepan, combine vinegar, water, sugar, salt, and mustard seeds. Heat until dissolved.
2. **Pack the Brussels Sprouts**
   Place Brussels sprouts in a jar.
3. **Add the Brine**
   Pour the hot brine over the Brussels sprouts.
4. **Cool and Refrigerate**
   Let cool, then refrigerate for at least 24 hours before serving.

Quick Pickled Cherries

Ingredients:

- 2 cups pitted cherries
- 1 cup apple cider vinegar
- 1/2 cup water
- 1/2 cup sugar
- 1 teaspoon salt
- 1 cinnamon stick (optional)

Instructions:

1. **Prepare the Brine**
   In a saucepan, combine vinegar, water, sugar, salt, and cinnamon stick. Heat until dissolved.
2. **Pack the Cherries**
   Place pitted cherries in a jar.
3. **Add the Brine**
   Pour the hot brine over the cherries.
4. **Cool and Refrigerate**
   Let cool, then refrigerate for at least 2 hours before serving.

Pickled Carrots and Daikon

Ingredients:

- 1 cup julienned carrots
- 1 cup julienned daikon radish
- 1 cup white vinegar
- 1/2 cup water
- 1/4 cup sugar
- 1 teaspoon salt
- 1 teaspoon chili flakes (optional)

Instructions:

1. **Prepare the Brine**
   In a saucepan, combine vinegar, water, sugar, salt, and chili flakes. Heat until dissolved.
2. **Pack the Vegetables**
   Place carrots and daikon in a jar.
3. **Add the Brine**
   Pour the hot brine over the vegetables.
4. **Cool and Refrigerate**
   Let cool, then refrigerate for at least 2 hours before serving.

Quick Pickled Ginger

Ingredients:

- 1 cup fresh ginger, thinly sliced
- 1 cup rice vinegar
- 1/2 cup sugar
- 1/2 teaspoon salt

Instructions:

1. **Prepare the Brine**
   In a saucepan, combine vinegar, sugar, and salt. Heat until dissolved.
2. **Pack the Ginger**
   Place sliced ginger in a jar.
3. **Add the Brine**
   Pour the hot brine over the ginger.
4. **Cool and Refrigerate**
   Let cool, then refrigerate for at least 1 hour before serving.

Pickled Shrimp

Ingredients:

- 1 pound shrimp, peeled and deveined
- 1 cup white vinegar
- 1/2 cup water
- 1 tablespoon sugar
- 1 tablespoon salt
- 1 teaspoon Old Bay seasoning (optional)

Instructions:

1. **Prepare the Brine**
   In a saucepan, combine vinegar, water, sugar, salt, and Old Bay seasoning. Heat until dissolved.
2. **Cook the Shrimp**
   Boil shrimp until pink, about 2-3 minutes. Drain and let cool.
3. **Pack the Shrimp**
   Place cooled shrimp in a jar.
4. **Add the Brine**
   Pour the hot brine over the shrimp.
5. **Cool and Refrigerate**
   Let cool, then refrigerate for at least 24 hours before serving.

Quick Pickled Apples

Ingredients:

- 2 cups thinly sliced apples
- 1 cup apple cider vinegar
- 1/2 cup water
- 1/4 cup sugar
- 1 teaspoon salt
- 1 teaspoon cinnamon (optional)

Instructions:

1. **Prepare the Brine**
   In a saucepan, combine vinegar, water, sugar, salt, and cinnamon. Heat until dissolved.
2. **Pack the Apples**
   Place sliced apples in a jar.
3. **Add the Brine**
   Pour the hot brine over the apples.
4. **Cool and Refrigerate**
   Let cool, then refrigerate for at least 1 hour before serving.

Pickled Fennel

Ingredients:

- 2 cups thinly sliced fennel
- 1 cup white vinegar
- 1/2 cup water
- 1 tablespoon sugar
- 1 teaspoon salt
- 1 teaspoon coriander seeds (optional)

Instructions:

1. **Prepare the Brine**
   In a saucepan, combine vinegar, water, sugar, salt, and coriander seeds. Heat until dissolved.
2. **Pack the Fennel**
   Place sliced fennel in a jar.
3. **Add the Brine**
   Pour the hot brine over the fennel.
4. **Cool and Refrigerate**
   Let cool, then refrigerate for at least 24 hours before serving.

Quick Pickled Lemons

Ingredients:

- 4 lemons, thinly sliced
- 1 cup lemon juice
- 1 cup water
- 1/2 cup sugar
- 1 tablespoon salt
- 1 teaspoon black peppercorns (optional)

Instructions:

1. **Prepare the Brine**
   In a saucepan, combine lemon juice, water, sugar, salt, and black peppercorns. Heat until dissolved.
2. **Pack the Lemons**
   Place lemon slices in a jar.
3. **Add the Brine**
   Pour the hot brine over the lemons.
4. **Cool and Refrigerate**
   Let cool, then refrigerate for at least 24 hours before serving.

Pickled Eggplant

Ingredients:

- 1 medium eggplant, sliced
- 1 cup white vinegar
- 1/2 cup water
- 1/4 cup olive oil
- 2 cloves garlic, minced
- 1 teaspoon salt
- 1 teaspoon oregano (optional)

Instructions:

1. **Prepare the Brine**
   In a saucepan, combine vinegar, water, olive oil, garlic, salt, and oregano. Heat until dissolved.
2. **Pack the Eggplant**
   Place sliced eggplant in a jar.
3. **Add the Brine**
   Pour the hot brine over the eggplant.
4. **Cool and Refrigerate**
   Let cool, then refrigerate for at least 48 hours before serving.

Quick Pickled Bell Peppers

Ingredients:

- 2 cups sliced bell peppers (any color)
- 1 cup apple cider vinegar
- 1/2 cup water
- 1/4 cup sugar
- 1 teaspoon salt
- 1 teaspoon garlic powder (optional)

Instructions:

1. **Prepare the Brine**
   In a saucepan, combine vinegar, water, sugar, salt, and garlic powder. Heat until dissolved.
2. **Pack the Bell Peppers**
   Place sliced bell peppers in a jar.
3. **Add the Brine**
   Pour the hot brine over the bell peppers.
4. **Cool and Refrigerate**
   Let cool, then refrigerate for at least 1 hour before serving.

Pickled Okra

Ingredients:

- 1 pound fresh okra, trimmed
- 1 cup white vinegar
- 1/2 cup water
- 1 tablespoon salt
- 1 tablespoon dill seeds (optional)
- 2 cloves garlic (optional)

Instructions:

1. **Prepare the Brine**
   In a saucepan, combine vinegar, water, salt, dill seeds, and garlic. Heat until dissolved.
2. **Pack the Okra**
   Place okra in a jar.
3. **Add the Brine**
   Pour the hot brine over the okra.
4. **Cool and Refrigerate**
   Let cool, then refrigerate for at least 48 hours before serving.

Quick Pickled Celery

Ingredients:

- 2 cups sliced celery
- 1 cup white vinegar
- 1/2 cup water
- 1/4 cup sugar
- 1 teaspoon salt
- 1 teaspoon red pepper flakes (optional)

Instructions:

1. **Prepare the Brine**
   In a saucepan, combine vinegar, water, sugar, salt, and red pepper flakes. Heat until dissolved.
2. **Pack the Celery**
   Place sliced celery in a jar.
3. **Add the Brine**
   Pour the hot brine over the celery.
4. **Cool and Refrigerate**
   Let cool, then refrigerate for at least 2 hours before serving.

Pickled Dill Carrots

Ingredients:

- 2 cups sliced carrots
- 1 cup white vinegar
- 1/2 cup water
- 1/4 cup sugar
- 1 teaspoon salt
- 1 tablespoon dill (fresh or dried)

Instructions:

1. **Prepare the Brine**
   In a saucepan, combine vinegar, water, sugar, salt, and dill. Heat until dissolved.
2. **Pack the Carrots**
   Place sliced carrots in a jar.
3. **Add the Brine**
   Pour the hot brine over the carrots.
4. **Cool and Refrigerate**
   Let cool, then refrigerate for at least 24 hours before serving.

Quick Pickled Pineapple

Ingredients:

- 2 cups fresh pineapple, cut into chunks
- 1 cup apple cider vinegar
- 1/2 cup water
- 1/4 cup sugar
- 1 teaspoon salt
- 1 teaspoon ginger (fresh or powdered, optional)

Instructions:

1. **Prepare the Brine**
   In a saucepan, combine vinegar, water, sugar, salt, and ginger. Heat until dissolved.
2. **Pack the Pineapple**
   Place pineapple chunks in a jar.
3. **Add the Brine**
   Pour the hot brine over the pineapple.
4. **Cool and Refrigerate**
   Let cool, then refrigerate for at least 2 hours before serving.

Pickled Baby Corn

Ingredients:

- 2 cups baby corn, whole
- 1 cup white vinegar
- 1/2 cup water
- 1/4 cup sugar
- 1 tablespoon salt
- 1 teaspoon mustard seeds (optional)

Instructions:

1. **Prepare the Brine**
   In a saucepan, combine vinegar, water, sugar, salt, and mustard seeds. Heat until dissolved.
2. **Pack the Baby Corn**
   Place baby corn in a jar.
3. **Add the Brine**
   Pour the hot brine over the baby corn.
4. **Cool and Refrigerate**
   Let cool, then refrigerate for at least 24 hours before serving.

Quick Pickled Artichokes

Ingredients:

- 2 cups canned or jarred artichoke hearts, drained
- 1 cup red wine vinegar
- 1/2 cup water
- 1/4 cup olive oil
- 1 tablespoon salt
- 2 cloves garlic, minced
- 1 teaspoon oregano (optional)

Instructions:

1. **Prepare the Brine**
   In a saucepan, combine vinegar, water, olive oil, salt, garlic, and oregano. Heat until dissolved.
2. **Pack the Artichokes**
   Place artichoke hearts in a jar.
3. **Add the Brine**
   Pour the hot brine over the artichokes.
4. **Cool and Refrigerate**
   Let cool, then refrigerate for at least 48 hours before serving.

Pickled Scallions

Ingredients:

- 1 bunch scallions, trimmed
- 1 cup rice vinegar
- 1/2 cup water
- 1/4 cup sugar
- 1 tablespoon salt

Instructions:

1. **Prepare the Brine**
   In a saucepan, combine rice vinegar, water, sugar, and salt. Heat until dissolved.
2. **Pack the Scallions**
   Place scallions in a jar.
3. **Add the Brine**
   Pour the hot brine over the scallions.
4. **Cool and Refrigerate**
   Let cool, then refrigerate for at least 1 hour before serving.

Quick Pickled Thai Basil

Ingredients:

- 1 cup fresh Thai basil leaves
- 1 cup rice vinegar
- 1/2 cup water
- 1/4 cup sugar
- 1 tablespoon salt

Instructions:

1. **Prepare the Brine**
   In a saucepan, combine rice vinegar, water, sugar, and salt. Heat until dissolved.
2. **Pack the Thai Basil**
   Place Thai basil leaves in a jar.
3. **Add the Brine**
   Pour the hot brine over the basil leaves.
4. **Cool and Refrigerate**
   Let cool, then refrigerate for at least 30 minutes before serving.

Pickled Radish Slaw

Ingredients:

- 2 cups shredded radish
- 1 cup apple cider vinegar
- 1/2 cup water
- 1/4 cup sugar
- 1 tablespoon salt
- 1 teaspoon sesame seeds (optional)

Instructions:

1. **Prepare the Brine**
   In a saucepan, combine apple cider vinegar, water, sugar, and salt. Heat until dissolved.
2. **Pack the Radish**
   Place shredded radish in a jar.
3. **Add the Brine**
   Pour the hot brine over the radish.
4. **Cool and Refrigerate**
   Let cool, then refrigerate for at least 1 hour before serving.

Quick Pickled Snow Peas

Ingredients:

- 2 cups snow peas, trimmed
- 1 cup rice vinegar
- 1/2 cup water
- 1/4 cup sugar
- 1 tablespoon salt
- 1 teaspoon crushed red pepper flakes (optional)

Instructions:

1. **Prepare the Brine**
   In a saucepan, combine rice vinegar, water, sugar, salt, and crushed red pepper flakes. Heat until dissolved.
2. **Pack the Snow Peas**
   Place snow peas in a jar.
3. **Add the Brine**
   Pour the hot brine over the snow peas.
4. **Cool and Refrigerate**
   Let cool, then refrigerate for at least 30 minutes before serving.

Pickled Baby Beets

Ingredients:

- 2 cups cooked baby beets, sliced
- 1 cup apple cider vinegar
- 1/2 cup water
- 1/4 cup sugar
- 1 tablespoon salt
- 1 teaspoon dill seeds (optional)

Instructions:

1. **Prepare the Brine**
   In a saucepan, combine apple cider vinegar, water, sugar, salt, and dill seeds. Heat until dissolved.
2. **Pack the Baby Beets**
   Place sliced baby beets in a jar.
3. **Add the Brine**
   Pour the hot brine over the beets.
4. **Cool and Refrigerate**
   Let cool, then refrigerate for at least 24 hours before serving.

Quick Pickled Cabbage

Ingredients:

- 4 cups shredded cabbage
- 1 cup white vinegar
- 1/2 cup water
- 1/4 cup sugar
- 1 tablespoon salt
- 1 teaspoon caraway seeds (optional)

Instructions:

1. **Prepare the Brine**
   In a saucepan, combine vinegar, water, sugar, salt, and caraway seeds. Heat until dissolved.
2. **Pack the Cabbage**
   Place shredded cabbage in a jar.
3. **Add the Brine**
   Pour the hot brine over the cabbage.
4. **Cool and Refrigerate**
   Let cool, then refrigerate for at least 1 hour before serving.

Pickled Cilantro Lime Carrots

Ingredients:

- 2 cups carrots, sliced
- 1 cup lime juice
- 1/2 cup water
- 1/4 cup sugar
- 1 tablespoon salt
- 1/2 cup fresh cilantro, chopped

Instructions:

1. **Prepare the Brine**
   In a saucepan, combine lime juice, water, sugar, and salt. Heat until dissolved.
2. **Pack the Carrots**
   Place sliced carrots and chopped cilantro in a jar.
3. **Add the Brine**
   Pour the hot brine over the carrots and cilantro.
4. **Cool and Refrigerate**
   Let cool, then refrigerate for at least 2 hours before serving.

Quick Pickled Green Beans

Ingredients:

- 2 cups green beans, trimmed
- 1 cup white vinegar
- 1/2 cup water
- 1/4 cup sugar
- 1 tablespoon salt
- 2 cloves garlic, smashed

Instructions:

1. **Prepare the Brine**
   In a saucepan, combine vinegar, water, sugar, salt, and garlic. Heat until dissolved.
2. **Pack the Green Beans**
   Place green beans in a jar.
3. **Add the Brine**
   Pour the hot brine over the green beans.
4. **Cool and Refrigerate**
   Let cool, then refrigerate for at least 24 hours before serving.

Pickled Sweet Potatoes

Ingredients:

- 2 cups sweet potatoes, peeled and sliced
- 1 cup apple cider vinegar
- 1/2 cup water
- 1/4 cup sugar
- 1 tablespoon salt
- 1 teaspoon cinnamon (optional)

Instructions:

1. **Prepare the Brine**
   In a saucepan, combine apple cider vinegar, water, sugar, salt, and cinnamon. Heat until dissolved.
2. **Pack the Sweet Potatoes**
   Place sweet potato slices in a jar.
3. **Add the Brine**
   Pour the hot brine over the sweet potatoes.
4. **Cool and Refrigerate**
   Let cool, then refrigerate for at least 48 hours before serving.

Quick Pickled Mustard Greens

Ingredients:

- 2 cups mustard greens, chopped
- 1 cup rice vinegar
- 1/2 cup water
- 1/4 cup sugar
- 1 tablespoon salt
- 1 teaspoon sesame oil (optional)

Instructions:

1. **Prepare the Brine**
   In a saucepan, combine rice vinegar, water, sugar, salt, and sesame oil. Heat until dissolved.
2. **Pack the Mustard Greens**
   Place chopped mustard greens in a jar.
3. **Add the Brine**
   Pour the hot brine over the mustard greens.
4. **Cool and Refrigerate**
   Let cool, then refrigerate for at least 1 hour before serving.

Pickled Daikon

Ingredients:

- 2 cups daikon radish, sliced
- 1 cup rice vinegar
- 1/2 cup water
- 1/4 cup sugar
- 1 tablespoon salt
- 1 teaspoon chili flakes (optional)

Instructions:

1. **Prepare the Brine**
   In a saucepan, combine rice vinegar, water, sugar, salt, and chili flakes. Heat until dissolved.
2. **Pack the Daikon**
   Place sliced daikon in a jar.
3. **Add the Brine**
   Pour the hot brine over the daikon.
4. **Cool and Refrigerate**
   Let cool, then refrigerate for at least 1 hour before serving.

Quick Pickled Lemongrass

Ingredients:

- 1 cup lemongrass, sliced
- 1 cup white vinegar
- 1/2 cup water
- 1/4 cup sugar
- 1 tablespoon salt

Instructions:

1. **Prepare the Brine**
   In a saucepan, combine vinegar, water, sugar, and salt. Heat until dissolved.
2. **Pack the Lemongrass**
   Place sliced lemongrass in a jar.
3. **Add the Brine**
   Pour the hot brine over the lemongrass.
4. **Cool and Refrigerate**
   Let cool, then refrigerate for at least 30 minutes before serving.

Pickled Fiddleheads

Ingredients:

- 2 cups fiddleheads, cleaned
- 1 cup white vinegar
- 1/2 cup water
- 1/4 cup sugar
- 1 tablespoon salt
- 2 cloves garlic, smashed
- 1 teaspoon mustard seeds (optional)

Instructions:

1. **Prepare the Brine**
   In a saucepan, combine vinegar, water, sugar, salt, garlic, and mustard seeds. Heat until dissolved.
2. **Pack the Fiddleheads**
   Place fiddleheads in a jar.
3. **Add the Brine**
   Pour the hot brine over the fiddleheads.
4. **Cool and Refrigerate**
   Let cool, then refrigerate for at least 48 hours before serving.

Quick Pickled Habaneros

Ingredients:

- 1 cup habanero peppers, sliced
- 1 cup white vinegar
- 1/2 cup water
- 1/4 cup sugar
- 1 tablespoon salt

Instructions:

1. **Prepare the Brine**
   In a saucepan, combine vinegar, water, sugar, and salt. Heat until dissolved.
2. **Pack the Habaneros**
   Place sliced habaneros in a jar.
3. **Add the Brine**
   Pour the hot brine over the habaneros.
4. **Cool and Refrigerate**
   Let cool, then refrigerate for at least 1 hour before serving.

Pickled Turnips

Ingredients:

- 2 cups turnips, sliced
- 1 cup rice vinegar
- 1/2 cup water
- 1/4 cup sugar
- 1 tablespoon salt
- 1 teaspoon coriander seeds (optional)

Instructions:

1. **Prepare the Brine**
   In a saucepan, combine rice vinegar, water, sugar, salt, and coriander seeds. Heat until dissolved.
2. **Pack the Turnips**
   Place sliced turnips in a jar.
3. **Add the Brine**
   Pour the hot brine over the turnips.
4. **Cool and Refrigerate**
   Let cool, then refrigerate for at least 24 hours before serving.

Quick Pickled Mango

Ingredients:

- 2 cups green mango, sliced
- 1 cup apple cider vinegar
- 1/2 cup water
- 1/4 cup sugar
- 1 tablespoon salt
- 1 teaspoon chili powder (optional)

Instructions:

1. **Prepare the Brine**
   In a saucepan, combine apple cider vinegar, water, sugar, salt, and chili powder. Heat until dissolved.
2. **Pack the Mango**
   Place mango slices in a jar.
3. **Add the Brine**
   Pour the hot brine over the mango.
4. **Cool and Refrigerate**
   Let cool, then refrigerate for at least 2 hours before serving.

Pickled Seaweed

Ingredients:

- 2 cups seaweed (wakame or dulse), rehydrated
- 1 cup rice vinegar
- 1/2 cup water
- 1/4 cup sugar
- 1 tablespoon salt
- 1 teaspoon sesame oil (optional)

Instructions:

1. **Prepare the Brine**
   In a saucepan, combine rice vinegar, water, sugar, salt, and sesame oil. Heat until dissolved.
2. **Pack the Seaweed**
   Place rehydrated seaweed in a jar.
3. **Add the Brine**
   Pour the hot brine over the seaweed.
4. **Cool and Refrigerate**
   Let cool, then refrigerate for at least 1 hour before serving.

Quick Pickled Cabbage and Carrots

Ingredients:

- 2 cups cabbage, shredded
- 1 cup carrots, shredded
- 1 cup white vinegar
- 1/2 cup water
- 1/4 cup sugar
- 1 tablespoon salt

Instructions:

1. **Prepare the Brine**
   In a saucepan, combine vinegar, water, sugar, and salt. Heat until dissolved.
2. **Pack the Cabbage and Carrots**
   Place shredded cabbage and carrots in a jar.
3. **Add the Brine**
   Pour the hot brine over the cabbage and carrots.
4. **Cool and Refrigerate**
   Let cool, then refrigerate for at least 1 hour before serving.

Pickled Coconut

Ingredients:

- 2 cups young coconut, sliced
- 1 cup rice vinegar
- 1/2 cup water
- 1/4 cup sugar
- 1 tablespoon salt

Instructions:

1. **Prepare the Brine**
   In a saucepan, combine rice vinegar, water, sugar, and salt. Heat until dissolved.
2. **Pack the Coconut**
   Place coconut slices in a jar.
3. **Add the Brine**
   Pour the hot brine over the coconut.
4. **Cool and Refrigerate**
   Let cool, then refrigerate for at least 24 hours before serving.

Quick Pickled Summer Squash

Ingredients:

- 2 cups summer squash, sliced
- 1 cup white vinegar
- 1/2 cup water
- 1/4 cup sugar
- 1 tablespoon salt
- 1 teaspoon dill (optional)

Instructions:

1. **Prepare the Brine**
   In a saucepan, combine vinegar, water, sugar, salt, and dill. Heat until dissolved.
2. **Pack the Summer Squash**
   Place summer squash slices in a jar.
3. **Add the Brine**
   Pour the hot brine over the summer squash.
4. **Cool and Refrigerate**
   Let cool, then refrigerate for at least 2 hours before serving.